CAMBRIDGE ASSIGNMENTS IN MUSIC

Form and Design

ROY BENNETT

CAMBRIDGE
UNIVERSITY PRESS

Contents

3

1

What is 'form' in music?

When a composer is writing a piece of music, he must plan his work every bit as carefully as an architect designing a building. In each case, the finished work must have continuity, balance, and shape – or *form*. But whereas architecture is concerned with a balance in space, music is a balance in time. In music, we use the word 'form' to describe the way in which a composer achieves this balance by arranging and setting in order his musical ideas – the way in which he designs and builds up his music.

We can think of the form of a piece of music as being the overall structure of the piece. But the composer must clothe this basic structure with interesting detail, and to do this he uses a variety of musical materials.

Repetition and contrast

Even in a fairly short piece, a composer rarely finds that one musical idea is enough. But too many ideas, following each other in haphazard fashion, would make his music appear to wander aimlessly and without purpose – to lack shape or form. So he must aim at a careful balance between the two basic ingredients of all musical forms and designs: repetition and contrast.

Some repetition of musical ideas is necessary in order to bind the music together – to bring unity to the piece. Some tunes may be heard twice, or even more, during a piece. Think of these as 'musical landmarks' to help you find your way around the music.

It is also very important, however, for the composer to introduce contrasting ideas so that his music has variety and interest. He can do this in several ways. The most likely, of course, is that he will bring in a completely new tune. But there are other ways of making musical contrasts, including change of key, mode (the contrast of major with minor), rhythm, pace, dynamics (louds and softs), mood, texture and timbre (or instrumental tone-colour). A composer may use only one of these at a time, or he may use several, depending upon how striking a contrast he wishes it to be.

Keys, scales and chords

One of the most important factors in building up a piece of music is the way in which the composer plans a balanced key-scheme. The key in which a piece of music begins is called the *tonic key*. This is the 'home' key – the *key-centre* for the whole piece. Although there may be several changes of key, the music will return 'home' to this key at the end of the piece.

Each key, whether major or minor, is based upon a scale of eight notes. Let us take, for example, a piece written in the key of C major. The notes of the scale will be:

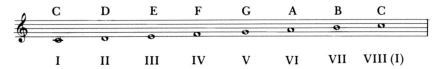

The first step of the scale is itself called the *tonic*; and each of the other steps has its own special name:

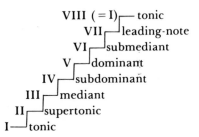

So if the piece is in C major, we call C major the tonic key. The tonic note is C; the supertonic is D; the mediant E; and so on.

A chord can be built upon any note of a scale. We refer to each chord by the same name as the step of the scale upon which it is built. Here are the three most important chords of the key of C major:

tonic chord: (built on the tonic note: C) 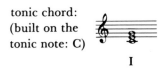 I	dominant chord: (built on the dominant note: G) V(7)	subdominant chord: (built on the subdominant note: F) IV

Here is a chart showing the most often used key signatures. In each case, the white note represents the tonic note of the major key; the black note represents the tonic note of its relative minor – the minor key which shares the same key signature. The leading-note of each minor key is shown in brackets. (In a minor key, the leading-note is extra to the key signature and, where necessary, must be shown in the music as an 'accidental'.)

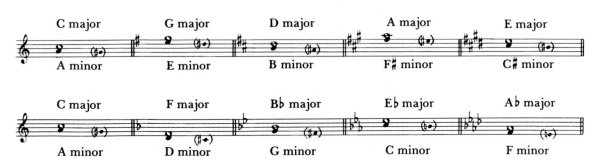

Assignment 1

Choose other keys besides C major as tonic keys. For each key:
Write out the scale with the correct key signature, and add roman numerals beneath the notes.
Give the letter-names of the notes which are
  (i) the tonic;   (iii) the subdominant;
  (ii) the dominant;   (iv) the leading-note.

Phrases and sentences These are the basic musical 'components' from which a composer builds a tune. The most usual length for a musical phrase is four bars, though phrases of eight bars, two bars, or even a single bar, are also quite common. Phrases consisting of an odd number of bars, such as three or five, are relatively rare.

Sing or play this well-known tune, which is built from four-bar and two-bar phrases:

'Early one morning'

English folk-song

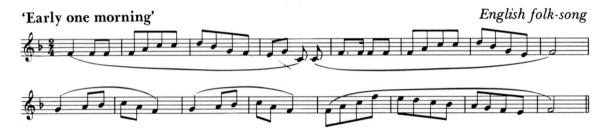

A musical sentence is most frequently eight bars in length, and is built from two or more phrases:

'Choral' Symphony

Beethoven

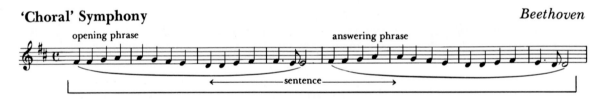

Cadences The endings of phrases and sentences are marked by cadences (from a Latin word *cadere,* meaning 'to fall'). Cadences in a piece of music are 'resting-points' - a kind of musical 'punctuation'. A cadence consists of a progression of two chords. There are four kinds of cadence:

Perfect cadence (or full-close). The two chords which make up this cadence are the dominant (V) and the tonic (I). A perfect cadence gives the music a sense of completion, of finality. Its effect is similar to that of a full-stop.

[tonic key: G major]

6

Plagal cadence. This consists of the chord of the subdominant (IV) followed by the tonic (I), and is another kind of musical full-stop. It is sometimes called an 'Amen' cadence as it is frequently used to harmonise this word at the end of hymns.

[tonic key: B♭ major]

IV   I

Imperfect cadence (or half-close). As its name suggests, this cadence makes the music at the point where it is used sound unfinished, incomplete. Its effect is that of a musical comma. An imperfect cadence consists of the progression of almost any chord - but frequently the tonic (I), the supertonic (II), or the subdominant (IV) - followed by the dominant chord (V).

[tonic key: D major]

I   V

Interrupted cadence (or 'surprise' cadence). This is quite easy to recognise since, as the name suggests, the music sounds interrupted. The composer leads us to expect a perfect cadence (V-I), but instead of the dominant chord being followed by the expected tonic, the ear is surprised by the music coming to rest on a quite different chord instead: usually the submediant (VI) (though it may be a chromatic chord to heighten the 'surprise').

'Wachet auf!' (Sleepers Wake!)

Bach

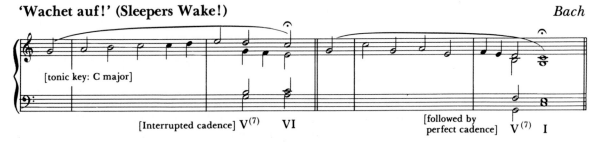

[tonic key: C major]

[Interrupted cadence] V$^{(7)}$ VI   [followed by perfect cadence] V$^{(7)}$ I

ℐssignment 2

Play or sing these tunes and identify the cadence which marks the end of each phrase:

'Barbara Allen'
'The British Grenadiers'
'Ye Banks and Braes'
'The First Nowell'
'Good King Wenceslas'

(All these tunes will be found in *The New National Song Book*.)

Modulation One of the most important ingredients in building up a piece of music is *modulation,* or change of key. In a very short, simple piece there may be no modulation at all; but a longer piece would sound very dull without some change of key to add interest and variety.

If we take again as an example a piece beginning in C major, we call C major the tonic key. If the music modulates to the key of G major, five notes higher than the tonic (remember always to include the lowest note when counting), then we call this a modulation to the dominant key.

Of course, a composer is free to modulate to any key he may choose; but for whichever key he selects as his tonic key (his key-centre) there is a handful of other keys which are closely related, so that modulation between these keys will sound particularly smooth and natural.

If the tonic is a *major* key, the most natural and therefore most likely modulation is to the dominant. Two other closely related keys are the relative minor (which shares the same key signature as the tonic major), and the subdominant major. Another common change of key is to the tonic minor (the minor key which shares the same tonic note as the tonic major key).

Here are the most closely related keys to a major tonic or key-centre, taking the key of C major as an example:

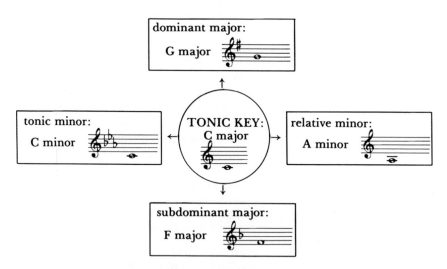

Two other keys closely related to a major tonic are the super-tonic minor (the relative minor of the subdominant), and the mediant minor (the relative minor of the dominant).

If the tonic is a *minor* key, the most natural modulation will be to the relative major (the major key which shares the same key signature as the tonic minor) or to the dominant minor. Another possible change of key is to the tonic major (the major key which shares the same tonic note as the tonic minor key).

Here are the most closely related keys to a minor tonic or key-centre, taking the key of C minor as an example:

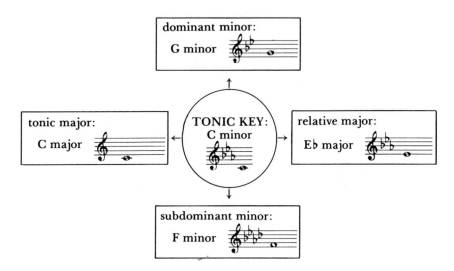

Two other keys closely related to a minor tonic are the relative major keys of both the subdominant minor and the dominant minor.

In every musical form or design, cadences, modulation and key schemes play a very important part in building up the music. In an examination, you may be asked to identify the various changes of key in a piece of music. The thing to do is to discover first of all which key, major or minor, is the tonic key of the piece. Think of this as the key-centre around which the related keys will revolve. Then be aware of which changes of key are most likely to occur, and look out for them.

Assignment 3

For practice, make similar diagrams to these two pages, but choosing other tonics as key-centres and showing the most closely related keys to each one.

2 Binary form

There are two simple forms or designs which composers use to shape fairly short pieces of music. One is called *binary*; the other is called *ternary*.

A piece in binary form divides into *two* sections (*bi*-nary, meaning two as in bicycle, or binoculars). We call these two sections A and B. Each of them is usually marked with repeat signs.

Listen to this music by Handel:

Minuet from *Music for the Royal Fireworks*　　　　　　　*Handel (1685-1759)*

The music clearly divides into two sections. Handel's plan for this piece is:

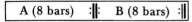

| A (8 bars) :‖: B (8 bars) :‖ |

A ends with an imperfect cadence in the tonic key, which makes the music at this point sound unfinished, suspended in mid-air. We feel that there is more music to come. B is clearly needed to complete the piece - ending with a perfect cadence in the tonic key - and also to balance A. We can think of the general shape of a piece in binary form as being rather like an arch:

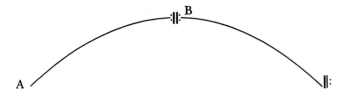

This arch-shape - and the need for A to be completed and balanced by B - is made much stronger if the music modulates, or changes key, at the end of A.

If the tonic is a major key, modulation at the end of A will usually be to the dominant key. In this lively March by Purcell, A fixes the tonic key (C major) firmly in mind, then modulates to the dominant key (G major). We enjoy this change of key, but at the same time we feel a need for the music to return 'home' to the tonic key during B.

March in C
Purcell (1659-1695)

If the tonic is a minor key, a likely modulation at the end of A
will be to the relative major (the major key which shares the
same key signature).

Pavane from an old French book of dances
Anon

The composer will sometimes build up part of section B by using a
sequence – a tuneful phrase immediately repeated, slightly higher
or lower in pitch. This sequence may be based upon an idea taken
from the music of section A.

In many binary pieces B is longer than A. This is often because
the composer takes the music of B through other related keys before
finally closing in the tonic key. The arch-shape will now be:

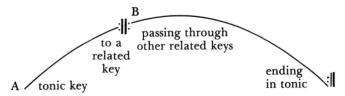

Although the arch-shape is no longer symmetrical, there is still a
balance of musical ideas between A and B. The tune which began A
is likely to be heard again at the beginning of B:

    perhaps inverted (turned upside down),

    or put down into the bass,

    or used to make a sequence,

    or merely transposed into the new key.

And the composer often neatly points the balance between A and B by
making the endings of the two sections similar, except for key.

Here is another march – one from a notebook of pieces which Bach composed for his wife, Anna Magdalena, when he was teaching her to play the harpsichord. Bach's plan for this piece is:

A (9 bars) :||: B (13 bars) :||

Notice how Bach uses *repetition* of certain musical ideas to point the balance between A and B: the same tune begins both sections, and the endings of the sections, imitating the trumpets and drums of the march, are alike except for key. But there is *contrast* as well: a contrast of texture between the crisp rhythm of the opening idea and later bars of flowing quavers; and the music explores a variety of contrasted keys, all closely related to the tonic, or key-centre, of D major.

March in D (from the Anna Magdalena Notebook)   *Bach (1685-1750)*

Assignment 4

Draw a diagram similar to those on pages 8 and 9, showing the most closely related keys if D major is the tonic, or key-centre. Which of these keys does Bach use in his March in D?

Notice that in each of these four pieces, both A and B are marked with repeat signs. We actually hear A A B B, but the music is printed A:‖: B:‖ so that basic form remains quite simply A B. As a general rule, remember that:

repeat signs never alter the form of a piece of music in any way.

Binary form was used a great deal in the 17th and 18th centuries, especially for dances, which composers often grouped together to make keyboard or orchestral *suites*. Since then, binary form has been rarely used except for short piano pieces or themes for sets of variations.

Checklist

Points to remember about binary form:

1. The music divides into *two* sections, each usually repeated:

2. A usually modulates away from the tonic key, and so sounds incomplete on its own.
3. B balances A, and completes the piece - working back to the tonic key, but usually passing through other related keys on the way.
4. Because of this, B is frequently longer than A.
5. B often begins with the same tune as A - either inverted, as a sequence, put down into the bass, or merely transposed into the new key.
6. The endings of A and B are often alike, except for key.
7. But in very simple binary pieces there may be little or no modulation, and little or no repetition of musical ideas.

Assignment 5

Song Tune   *Purcell (1659-1695)*

Purcell's plan for this binary piece is:

> A (8 bars) :||: B (8 bars) :||

1. Which key is the tonic, or key-centre, for this piece?
2. Which accidental, towards the end of A, shows that the music has changed key?
3. This accidental is the *leading-note* of the new key. Which key is it?
4. How is this new key related to the tonic key of the piece?
5. B begins with the same tune as A. Is the tune:
    (i)   inverted?
    (ii) put down into the bass?
    (iii) merely transposed into the new key?

Assignment 6

Minuet (composed at the age of five)   *Mozart (1756-1791)*

1. In which key is this music written?
2. Which accidental, towards the end of A, shows that the music has changed key?
3. This accidental is the leading-note of the new key, which is firmly fixed by a perfect cadence at the end of A. Which key is it?
4. How is this key related to the tonic key of the piece?

5. B begins with a sequence which lasts for 4 bars. Does this sequence rise, or fall?
6. Give the bar numbers where another sequence occurs.
7. In this short binary piece, Mozart makes sure that B balances and 'belongs' to A. At which bars are there similarities between them?
8. Write out a plan for this piece, using the letters A and B and repeat signs, and showing the number of bars in each section.

Assignment 7

Theme for variations from the 'Surprise' Symphony

Haydn (1732-1809)

1. What is the tonic key of this music?
2. Does A end with (i) an imperfect cadence in the tonic key?
   or (ii) a perfect cadence in the dominant key?
3. Which two bars of section B are similar to the opening of section A? In what way are they similar?
4. Which section of the orchestra plays the first part of this theme?
5. Haydn varies each repeat by changing the orchestration in some way. Describe the change in the accompaniment when A is repeated.
6. What change does Haydn make when B is repeated?

Assignment 8

Hornpipe from *The Water Music* (arr. Harty)

Handel (1685-1759)

1. Name the tonic key of this piece.
2. In which key, and with which kind of cadence, does A end?
3. There is a similarity between the beginning of A and the beginning of B. Is this a similarity of tune, of rhythm, or of key?
4. Choose an Italian term to match the pace of this music:
   andante; adagio; allegro; moderato.
5. Which instruments play each section the first time it is heard?
6. Which instruments join in the repeats?
7. Who would be most likely to dance a hornpipe?

Assignment 9

Sarabande from a Violin Sonata *Corelli (1653-1713)*

1. Is this music written in the major, or in the minor?
2. What is the tonic key for the piece?
3. Draw a diagram, similar to those on pages 8 and 9, to show the keys which are closely related to this tonic or key-centre.
4. Does A end with (i) a perfect cadence in the tonic key?
   (ii)   an imperfect cadence in the tonic key?
   (iii) a perfect cadence in the dominant key?
5. Through which key does the music pass in bars 9 to 10? How is this key related to the tonic?
6. Through which key does the music pass in bars 11 to 12? How is this key related to the tonic?
7. What musical term describes bars 9 to 12?
8. Choose an Italian term to match the speed of this music:
   largo; allegro; vivace; presto.
9. Which keyboard instrument plays the accompaniment in this 17th century violin sonata?
10. Which instrument is being used to strengthen the bass line?

Assignment 10

Minuet from Orchestral Suite No. 2 *Bach (1685-1750)*

1. What is the tonic key of this music?
2. Draw a diagram, similar to those on pages 8 and 9, to show the keys which are most closely related to this tonic or key-centre.
3. Does section A of this binary piece end with:
   (i) an imperfect cadence in the tonic key?

      (ii)   a perfect cadence in the dominant key?

      (iii)   a perfect cadence in the relative major?

4. In which key is the music at bar 16? How is this key related to the tonic key?

5. At bars 17-18, the music passes through the key of the subdominant minor. Which key is this?

6. What similarities are there between A and B in this binary piece?

7. Give the bar numbers where a sequence is heard.

8. Write out Bach's plan for this piece, using the letters A and B and repeat signs, and showing the number of bars in each section.

9. Name the solo instrument which plays in this piece.

10. Which family of instruments plays the accompaniment?

11. What is a *suite*?

Assignment 11

Gavotte from Orchestral Suite No. 3

Bach (1685-1750)

1. Which key does Bach choose as his tonic for this Gavotte?

2. Draw a diagram, similar to those on pages 8 and 9, to show the keys which are most closely related to this tonic or key-centre.

3. Which accidental, towards the end of A, shows that the music has changed key?

4. What is the new key? How is it related to the tonic key?

5. The same tune is used to begin both A and B. How does Bach treat it at the beginning of B? Is it:

      (i)   inverted?

      (ii)   put down into the bass?

      (iii) merely transposed into the new key?

6. In which key is the music at bars 12 to 18? How is this key related to the tonic key?

7. In bars 18 to 20, the music passes through the key of the supertonic minor. Which key is this?

8. In which two bars of B does the music pass through the key of G major? How is this key related to the tonic?

9. Name the main instruments which Bach uses in this Gavotte.

10. Write out a plan to show the design of this binary piece, using the letters A and B and repeat signs, and showing the number of bars in each section.

3

Ternary form

A piece of music in *ternary* form divides into *three* sections – A B A – making a kind of 'musical sandwich':

A¹ statement	B contrast (an episode)	A² repetition

A^1 and A^2 use the same music. B presents a contrast in some way – the filling in the sandwich! We call B an *episode*, meaning a section which contrasts with the music heard before and after it, and which usually appears once only.

You will often find that A^1 ends with a perfect cadence in the tonic key, so that it sounds rather like a complete, short piece in itself. B is in a different key; and A^2 is in the tonic key again. When music A returns as A^2 in the third section of the piece, it may be exactly the same as when it was first heard, or the composer may decide to change it in some way to add more interest. But it will always be recognisable as a return of music A after the contrast of music B.

Here is a short piece in ternary form in which A and B are well contrasted, making it easy to tell when B begins, and when music A returns as A^2 later on. Schumann's plan for this piece is:

> A^1 (8 bars) D minor
> B (8 bars) D major — the tonic major
> A^2 (8 bars) D minor

Notice how Schumann varies the return of music A at the beginning of the third section (A^2) by giving the tune to the left hand.

Volksliedchen (Little Folk-Song)

Schumann (1810-1856)

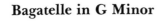 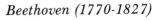

In Schumann's *Volksliedchen,* A and B have quite different tunes – but there are several other sharp contrasts as well:

Contrasts	Music A	Music B
mode:	D minor	D major
rhythm:	♩ ♩ 𝅗𝅥	♫♫♩ ♪
pace:	fairly slowly	slightly faster
dynamics:	*piano:* softly	*forte:* loudly
mood:	sad; in song style	joyful; more like a dance
texture:	*legato:* smoothly	*staccato:* crisp, detached

Now play or listen to this Bagatelle by Beethoven. The main contrasts between A and B are those of key, mode (minor/major), rhythm, and texture (A: a light *staccato;* B: a flowing *legato*).

Bagatelle in G Minor

Beethoven (1770-1827)

If A² is an exact repetition of A¹, then there is really no need for the composer to write out the music of A all over again. So you may find at the end of B the Italian words *da capo.* This means 'repeat again from the beginning', and you must then look for the word *fine,* meaning 'end here when the music is repeated'. What the composer is simply saying is 'after B, play A again', so in a ternary piece printed in this way the design is quite clear – *da capo* will be found at the end of B, and *fine* will mark the end of music A. The origin of this is found in many arias from operas and oratorios written during the 18th century. As A^2 was often an exact repetition of A^1, composers rarely bothered to write out the music of A again. Instead, they merely wrote *da capo* at the end of B. Arias written out in this way are called 'da capo arias'. (A good example is 'Why do the nations rage so furiously together?' from Handel's *Messiah*.)

Here is a Norwegian Dance by Grieg which can be printed in this way as A^2 is an exact repetition of A^1. Notice that Grieg uses the same tune for both A and B – but he brings in several striking contrasts so that we can easily distinguish between the sections.

Norwegian Dance No. 3

Grieg (1843-1907)

Assignment 12

When you have listened to Grieg's Norwegian Dance, make a list of contrasts between music A and music B. Make your list as detailed as you can.

Checklist

Points to remember about ternary form

1. The music divides into three sections: A^1 B A^2.
2. A^1 and A^2 are recognisably the same music. B is a contrast.
3. A^1 often ends with a perfect cadence in the tonic key. B is usually in a different key. A^2 is in the tonic key once more.
4. A^2 may be an exact repetition of A^1 or it may be varied in some way.
5. A *link* may be used to join sections smoothly together.
6. A^2 may be followed by a *coda*, or 'rounding-off'.
7. The music may be printed in abbreviated *da capo* layout.

Assignment 13

Night Watchman's Song
(composed after reading Shakespeare's play, *Macbeth*)

Grieg (1843-1907)

Molto Andante e semplice

1. Which key does Grieg choose as the tonic key for this piano piece?
2. In which key is the music at bar 10? (The accidental which appears is the leading-note of the new key.)
3. Does A end in the tonic, the dominant, or the relative minor?
4. Is the music of A: (i)   completely in unison?
                        (ii) in harmony throughout?
                        (iii) a mixture of both?
5. Is the music of B in the tonic minor, or the relative minor?
6. List the main contrasts presented by music B in this piece.
7. Suggest a word to describe the mood of music B.
8. Which changes does Grieg make when music A returns as A²?
9. Write out a plan or draw a diagram to show the design of this piece, using the letters A and B. Show the number of bars in each section.
10. What nationality was Grieg?
11. Name another piece of music composed by Grieg.

Assignment 14

Chanson Triste   Tchaikovsky (1840-1893)

Allegro non troppo

1. What is the tonic key of this music?
2. At which bar does section B begin in this ternary piece?
3. In which key is B? How is this key related to the tonic key?
4. Is the contrast between music A and music B mainly of tune, of rhythm, or of key?
5. What similarity is there between the tune of A and the tune of B?
6. What is the meaning of the Italian direction at the end of B?
7. Describe the mood of this music.
8. Which instrument plays the melody? Do you think this is a good instrument to choose to play this piece? Why?
9. Name any other pieces by Tchaikovsky which you have heard.

Assignment 15
Slow movement from Flute Quartet (K285) *Mozart (1756-1791)*

1. Which instruments take part in this Quartet?
2. What is meant by the pace marking *adagio?*
3. Mozart writes *sempre p* beneath the music of each instrument. What does he mean by this?
4. Which other Italian word would you expect to find beneath the music of the string parts in this piece?
5. In which minor key is this music written? (The main notes of bar 1 form an arpeggio of the tonic chord.)
6. At which bar does section B of this ternary piece begin? (A^1 closes firmly with a perfect cadence in the tonic key; B immediately follows.)
7. Is the music of section B in:
    (i)   the relative major?
    (ii) the dominant major?
8. Where does music A return as A^2? (Look carefully at the music of bars 1 and 2; then discover where this music returns approximately two-thirds of the way through the piece.)
9. In which bar does Mozart write a short link to join two sections smoothly together?
10. Do you think this music comes at the end of Mozart's Flute Quartet, or do you think there is more music to follow?

Assignment 16   Hungarian Dance No. 5   *Brahms (1833-1897)*

As a young man, Brahms met a young violinist called Reményi. The two of them travelled through Hungary giving concerts together, and it was in this way that Brahms was introduced to Hungarian gypsy music. He arranged several of the tunes he heard for piano duet. Later on, they were arranged for full orchestra.

1. In which key does section A begin?
2. At which bar does section B begin?
3. In which key is B?
4. The Italian directions *poco rit* and *in tempo* are used several times in this music. What do they mean?
5. In bars 35 and 39 there is a rest on the main beat followed by an accented note off the beat. Which musical term describes this exciting rhythmic effect?
6. Make a list of the contrasts which Brahms introduces during section B of this ternary piece.

Assignment 17 — Gavotte from the 'Classical' Symphony   *Prokofiev (1891-1953)*

Prokofiev wrote his first symphony in 1916 when he was twenty-five. He called it the 'Classical' because his aim was to compose a short symphony using 18th century forms, to be played by an orchestra of the same size as that used by Haydn and Mozart. The music has a great deal of the polish and elegance of the Classical period – but there are surprising changes of key and sudden twists of melody which give it a definite 20th century flavour.

1. At which bar does (i) section B begin?
                  (ii) music A return as A²?
2. In which key is music B? How is this related to the tonic key of D major?
3. Describe the accompaniment to the tune in section B.
4. Prokofiev makes his music more interesting by making several changes in music A when it returns as A². Listen to the music, carefully following the melody-line score; then describe these changes.
5. What nationality was Prokofiev?
6. Mention another piece of music which he composed.

Assignment 18

Tartars' Dance

Borodin (1833-1887)

This is one of the colourful Polovtsian Dances from the second act of Borodin's opera, *Prince Igor*. Igor has been captured by a barbaric tribe known as the Polovtsi; but their leader, Khan Konchak, treats his prisoner with great courtesy. Slave girls, prisoners and warriors entertain the Prince with dances and songs. In this ternary piece, music A is danced by fierce Tartar warriors; music B is a dance for the prisoners. Here are the opening bars of each section.

1. Which two sections of the orchestra provide most colour in music A?
2. Which section of the orchestra is most important at the beginning of music B?
3. Choose a dynamic marking for the beginning of each tune:
   p mf f ff
4. The tune of B is immediately repeated. What changes does Borodin make when it is played for the second time?
5. There are several striking contrasts in this piece between A and B. List as many of these as you can.
6. In spite of these contrasts, there is an important similarity between the beginning of A and the beginning of B. Is this a similarity of tune, of key, of rhythm, or of orchestration?
7. When music A returns as A², is it more or less the same as when it was first heard, or does Borodin make any important changes?
8. Name three percussion instruments which Borodin uses to bring colour and excitement to this barbaric dance.

Binary or Ternary?

In certain short pieces, it may be difficult to decide whether the form the composer is using to build up the music is binary or ternary. Play or listen to this Minuet by Haydn:

Haydn's Minuet is divided by a double bar and repeat signs into two parts. The first part modulates away from the tonic key of C major and comes to rest at the double bar on a perfect cadence in the dominant key of G major. So the first part depends upon the music following the double bar to balance and complete the piece, eventually returning 'home' to the tonic key. This seems to suggest the piece is in binary form with the plan:

A (8 bars) :‖: B (16 bars) :‖

But it could be argued that the final 8 bars are the same music as the first 8 bars - with 8 bars of different music in between. This suggests ternary form, with the plan:

A^1 (8 bars) :‖: B (8 bars) + A^2 (8 bars) :‖

(Remember that in neither case do the repeat signs make any difference to the actual form.)

Is a piece like this binary or ternary? Experienced musicians have always argued about this, so there is no clear-cut answer! Should you be given a piece like this in an examination, either answer will be acceptable provided you give good reasons for your choice. It is not the actual label 'binary' or 'ternary' which is most important, but the reasoning behind your answer.

Assignment 19

Listen again to Haydn's Minuet and decide which form is being used. Do you think it is binary, or ternary? Remember to give good reasons to support your choice. Some pointers to each form are given below – but refresh your memory about the details by looking again at the checklists on binary form (page 13) and ternary form (page 21).

Illustrate your answer by writing a plan or drawing a diagram to show the design of Haydn's piece. Include the letters A and B and repeat signs, and show the number of bars in each section.

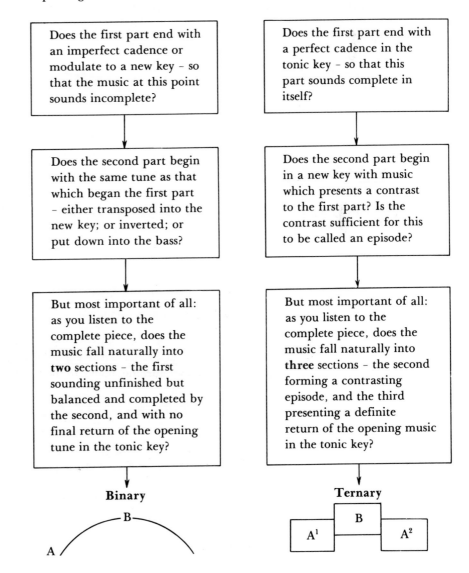

Does the first part end with an imperfect cadence or modulate to a new key – so that the music at this point sounds incomplete?	Does the first part end with a perfect cadence in the tonic key – so that this part sounds complete in itself?

| Does the second part begin with the same tune as that which began the first part – either transposed into the new key; or inverted; or put down into the bass? | Does the second part begin in a new key with music which presents a contrast to the first part? Is the contrast sufficient for this to be called an episode? |

| But most important of all: as you listen to the complete piece, does the music fall naturally into **two** sections – the first sounding unfinished but balanced and completed by the second, and with no final return of the opening tune in the tonic key? | But most important of all: as you listen to the complete piece, does the music fall naturally into **three** sections – the second forming a contrasting episode, and the third presenting a definite return of the opening music in the tonic key? |

Binary

Ternary

Assignment 20

Listen to each of these seven short pieces, carefully following the printed music. In some cases, you may find that the form the composer is using is clearly binary - or clearly ternary. In other cases it may not be quite so easy to decide! Refer to the main pointers to each form on page 29 but let your ear make the final decision. Does it accept two sections (binary), or three (ternary)?

For each piece:

1. Name the form the composer has used to build up his music – binary or ternary.
2. Give reasons to support your choice.
3. Make out a plan, or draw a diagram, clearly showing the design. Include the letters A and B and repeat signs, and show the number of bars in each section.

1 Siciliano: 'La Paix' from *Music for the Royal Fireworks*   Handel (1685-1759)

2 Minuet from String Quartet in A Major   *Hofstetter (?-1785)*

(Until recently, this String Quartet was thought to be by Haydn.)

3 Musette (from the Anna Magdalena Notebook)

Bach (1685-1750)

4 Waltz in A Flat

Brahms (1833-1897)

5 Gavotte: 'La Bourbonnoise'

Couperin (1668-1733)

6 Scherzo from the 'Moonlight' Sonata

Beethoven (1770-1827)

This music is the first page of a longer movement from the Sonata.
It took on the nickname of 'Moonlight' when a critic wrote that the
slow first movement reminded him of Lake Lucerne by moonlight.

7 'Anitra's Dance' from *Peer Gynt*

Grieg (1843-1907)

5

Minuet &
trio form

The minuet was a stately French dance, of moderate speed and with three beats to a bar, which became very popular at the court of Louis XIV, the 'Sun King', around the middle of the 17th century. Like many French fashions, it soon spread to other countries.

Minuets were often written in pairs – the second minuet making a contrast of some kind with the first. To make a longer piece, the two were performed in sandwich fashion:

> minuet I : minuet II : minuet I

The second minuet was usually in a new key, and frequently in the opposite mode – for instance, in the minor if the first minuet was in the major. As this second minuet was often scored for three instruments only, it became known as the *trio*. The custom was to omit any repeats in the first minuet when it was played again after the trio.

Here is the pair of contrasted minuets with which Handel concludes his *Music for the Royal Fireworks*. It is likely that he intended the second minuet – the trio – to be played by two oboes and a bassoon, but some conductors allow the strings to join in, or alternate, with the woodwind trio.

Minuets I and II from *Music for the Royal Fireworks*   *Handel (1685-1759)*

Minuet I

Minuet II

Other dances, such as bourrées and gavottes (and even pieces which were not dances at all) were written in pairs to be performed in this way. As the basic plan of such pieces was always the same, the name *minuet and trio* came to describe the form itself.

The overall shape of a piece in minuet and trio form is ternary:

A^1: minuet section — ending in the tonic key;
B : trio (minuet II) – a contrast, usually in a new key;
A^2: minuet section again – this time without repeats.

But each of these main sections - both the minuet and the trio - is
a complete binary or ternary design in itself:

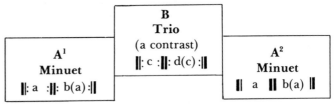

In the second half of the 18th century, composers included the
minuet - still with its contrasting trio - in instrumental works
such as symphonies and string quartets, and sometimes sonatas.

In the symphonies of Haydn and Mozart, the minuet is placed third
in the order of movements where it provides a contrast between the
slow second movement and the swift, more boisterous, finale.

Although the trio section is no longer written for three instruments
only, there is usually a marked change of orchestration -
often featuring solos for wind instruments - and a lightness of
texture to contrast with the fuller sound of the minuet section.

Minuet from Symphony No. 39 in E Flat   *Mozart (1756-1791)*

Haydn, in his later symphonies, increased the pace of the minuet and brought an earthy, out-door flavour to what had once been an elegant, courtly dance. Beethoven increased the pace still further, and eventually transformed the minuet into the brisk and vigorous *scherzo* – an Italian word meaning 'a joke'. Not all scherzos are humorous, but they are often dramatic in character and contain a strong element of surprise.

At first, like the minuet, the scherzo was written in three-time – but usually at such a swift pace that the music must be counted as one-in-a-bar. The design was exactly the same as a piece in minuet and trio form:

> scherzo : trio (a contrast) : scherzo (without repeats)

Play or listen to this Scherzo by Beethoven, then complete the assignment which follows.

Scherzo from Piano Sonata No. 15

Beethoven (1770-1827)

Trio

La seconda parte una volta

Scherzo da capo

Assignment 21

1. In which key is the main scherzo section?
2. In which key is the trio section? How is this key related to the key of the scherzo section?
3. In which form – binary, or ternary – is the scherzo section?
4. In which form is the trio section?
5. Instead of using repeat signs, Beethoven writes out the second part of the trio section in full. Why is this?
6. *Scherzo* is Italian for 'a joke'. Where, and how, does Beethoven introduce touches of humour into this music?
7. Beethoven's Piano Sonata No. 15 is in four movements, of which this Scherzo is the third. The second is in D minor with two beats to a bar, and marked *andante*. What contrasts would this Scherzo provide?
8. If you were to listen to a complete performance of this Sonata, what music would you expect to hear after the Trio?

Checklist

Points to remember about minuet and trio form:

1. The overall shape is ternary:
   A¹ (minuet)   :   B (trio)   :   A² (minuet again)
2. But each section is a complete binary or ternary design in itself.
3. The trio (originally for three instruments only) provides a contrast to the minuet section, and is usually in a new key.
4. The minuet section is played again after the trio – but this time without repeats.
5. In the second half of the 18th century (the time of Haydn and Mozart) the Minuet and Trio became the usual third movement of works such as the symphony and the string quartet. It also occurs in some sonatas.
6. It was transformed by Beethoven into the much brisker and more vigorous *Scherzo*.
7. Minuet and trio form may be used for movements and pieces which are not minuets or scherzos.

Assignment 22

Minuet from Piano Sonata No. 5   *Haydn (1732-1809)*

Menuetto da capo

1. Suggest an Italian word to indicate the pace of this music.
2. Which key does Haydn choose for the minuet section?
3. In which key is the trio section? How is this key related to the key of the minuet section?
4. In which form – binary, or ternary – is the minuet section?
5. In which form is the trio section?
6. Mention two ways in which the trio contrasts with the minuet.
7. Haydn composed most of his music during the second half of the 18th century. Would you describe this as Baroque, Classical or Romantic?
8. Name another composer who lived at the same time as Haydn.

Assignment 23

Third Movement from *Eine Kleine Nachtmusik*

Mozart (1756-1791)

1. *Eine Kleine Nachtmusik* is a *serenade*, meaning 'music to be played late in the evening'. Which instruments play this serenade?
2. In which key is the minuet section?
3. Is the trio section in the tonic major, the tonic minor, or the dominant?
4. In which form – binary, or ternary – is the minuet section?
5. In which from is the trio section?
6. The pace is *allegretto*. Is this faster, or slower, than *allegro*?
7. *Eine Kleine Nachtmusik* is in four movements of which this Minuet and Trio is the third. The second movement is a flowing *Romanze;* the final movement is a *Rondo.* In a complete performance of this serenade, what music would you expect to hear after the Trio?

Assignment 24

Scherzo from the 'Spring' Sonata

Beethoven (1770-1827)

Trio

Fine

D.C.

1. Which instruments play this music?
2. What is meant by the pace indication *allegro molto*?
3. Beethoven directs that the first part of this scherzo should be played without repeat. Why is this?
4. In which form – binary, or ternary – is the main scherzo section?
5. In which form is the trio section ?
6. Which contrasts are there between the scherzo section and the trio?
7. Scherzo means 'a joke'. What, do you think, does Beethoven intend to be the joke in this piece?

6

Special Assign- ment A

Each of these four pieces is in binary, ternary, or minuet and trio form. Your assignment here is to investigate each piece fully and to discover which form the composer has used to build up his music. A few clues have been scattered here and there to help you.

First, refresh your memory about the main points of each form by reading through the checklists on pages 13, 21, and 37.
Then listen to each piece, carefully following the melody-line score. Use your eyes and ears to help each other.

1. Note down all the important features of each piece, such as:
   (i)   bar numbers where sections begin and end;
   (ii) the key scheme used;
   (iii) any striking contrasts, or similarities, between sections;
   (iv) interesting choice of instruments; and so on.
2. Add as many important facts as you can about each composer.
3. Make out a plan, or draw a diagram, clearly showing the form of each piece, using the letters A, B and so on, and giving the bar numbers for each section.
4. Finally, organise your findings into a detailed report on each piece.

1 Badinerie from Orchestral Suite No. 2

Bach (1685-1750)

(crisp and lively)

2 Third Movement from Septet in E Flat

Beethoven (1770-1827)

3 'Carillon' from *L'Arlésienne* Suite 1

Bizet (1838-1875)

4 Allegro deciso from *The Water Music* (arr. Harty)   *Handel (1685-1759)*

7 Simple Rondo form

In a *rondo*, the main theme (A) keeps 'coming round', with contrasting sections (B, C, and so on) in between – like a 'double-decker' musical sandwich. These contrasting sections – the fillings in the sandwich – are called *episodes*. The main theme (A) begins and ends in the tonic key each time; each episode is in a related key. A plan for a simple rondo with two episodes looks like this:

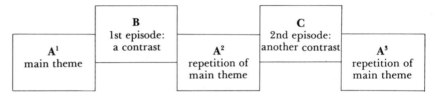

| A¹ main theme | B 1st episode: a contrast | A² repetition of main theme | C 2nd episode: another contrast | A³ repetition of main theme |

Notice that in writing a rondo, the composer is using the two basic ingredients of musical form and design: repetition and contrast. The repetitions of the main theme bind the music together and bring unity to the piece; the episodes present contrasts to hold the interest of the listener.

Some rondos have three, or even more, episodes. But there is a problem here – not that the composer will be unable to think up enough contrasting music for the episodes, but that by bringing round the main theme too many times he will risk boring the listener. (There is a rondo by the 17th century French composer, Couperin, in which the main theme comes round nine times.) So to keep the music interesting, the main theme (A) may be shortened or varied in some way when it returns.

In 17th century rondos, contrast between the sections may be slight, relying more upon changes of key than on introducing completely different tunes. Here is a very clearly designed rondo from the incidental music which Purcell composed for *The Fairy Queen* – an adaptation of Shakespeare's play *A Midsummer Night's Dream*. Purcell uses the French name 'rondeau' as a title.

Rondeau from *The Fairy Queen*   *Purcell (1659-1695)*

A¹   main theme in tonic key (B flat major):

B   first contrasting episode, modulating to dominant (F major):

A²   main theme again in tonic:

C   second contrasting episode, in relative minor (G minor):

A³   final appearance of main theme in tonic:

Composers after the 17th century use bolder musical contrasts
between the sections. A *link* may be used to join two sections
smoothly together; and the final appearance of A may be followed
by a *coda* to round off the piece.

Play or listen to this Rondo by Beethoven:

Rondo from a Sonatina for piano

Beethoven (1770-1827)

The music includes the following text markings within the score:

mf (bar 50), f (bar 55), p (bar 60), fz, ad libitum, p a tempo (bar 75), Link, (smoothly joining C to A³), (final appearance of main theme, complete, in tonic key), mf (bar 80), p, Coda (bar 90), p, f, (rounding off firmly in the tonic key)

Assignment 25
Checklist

Make out a detailed plan of the design of Beethoven's Rondo, using the letters A, B, and C, and showing the key used for each section.

Points to remember about simple rondo form

1. The plan for a simple rondo is A B A C A (D A . . . etc).
2. A begins and ends in the tonic key each time.
3. Each episode (B, C, and so on) is a contrast in a related key.
4. When the main theme (A) reappears, it may be shortened or varied in some way.
5. A *link* may be used to join sections smoothly together.
6. The final appearance of A may be followed by a *coda*.

Assignment 26

Prélude to *Carmen*

Bizet (1838-1875)

Here is an exciting orchestral piece by the French composer, Bizet.
It is a very clear example of a simple rondo, though it is known
by quite another name – the Prélude to his colourful opera, *Carmen*.
All the sections of this rondo are well contrasted – and it is very
easy to recognise the main rondo theme each time it comes round!

1. Listen to Bizet's music, carefully following the melody-line score. How many times in this rondo does the main theme (A) come round? Give the bar number for each appearance.
2. Is the main theme played *staccato* or *legato*?
3. Which percussion instrument adds colour and excitement to the main theme each time it is heard?
4. Which key does Bizet choose as his tonic key for this piece?
5. At which bar does the first episode (B) begin?
6. Is B in the tonic, the dominant, or the relative minor?
7. What are the main contrasts between the music of A and the music of B?
8. What name is given to the four bars, 31 to 34?
9. At which bar does the second episode (C) begin?
10. Is the music of episode C in a key closely related to the tonic or is it in a 'distant' key?
11. Which section of the orchestra accompanies the tune of music C when it is first played?
12. This tune is immediately repeated – but with several striking differences. List as many of these as you can.
13. Suggest another word instead of Prélude, to mean an orchestral piece played at the beginning of an opera.
14. Choose an Italian phrase to match the pace and mood of this music: *adagio lamentoso*; *allegro giocoso*; *andante cantabile*.
15. Orchestral pieces are sometimes arranged for piano solo or piano duet. Do you think such an arrangement of this music would be effective? Why?

Assignment 27

Gavotte: 'Les Moissoneurs' (The Harvesters) *Couperin (1668-1733)*

This is a lively peasant dance, designed as a simple rondo.

1. What is the tonic key for this piece?
2. At which bar does A¹ end?
3. Does A¹ end with (i)   an imperfect cadence in the tonic?
   (ii)   a perfect cadence in the tonic?
   (iii)   a perfect cadence in the dominant?
4. During the first episode (B) the music modulates to the key of F major. How is this key related to the tonic key?
5. At which bar does A return after section B?
6. Where does the second episode (C) begin? This episode is in the relative minor. Which key is this?
7. What is the main contrast between the music of episode C and the music of episode B? Is it a contrast of tune, of rhythm, or of key?
8. Some rondos have three, or even more, episodes. Is there a third episode (D) in this rondo? If so, where does it begin?

Assignment 28   **Rondo from Horn Concerto No. 3**   *Mozart (1756-1791)*

1. This rondo is from the third of a set of four concertos which Mozart composed for a keen and skilful horn player, called Leutgeb, who kept a cheese shop in Vienna. What is a concerto?
2. In which key is this music written?
3. How many times in this rondo does the main theme (A) come round? Give the bar number for each appearance.
4. Where does section B begin? How does this episode contrast with the main rondo theme?
5. Where does section C begin? In which key is this episode? How is it related to the tonic key?
6. Describe in detail how Mozart uses his soloist and orchestra to build up the music of section C.
7. Is there a section D in this rondo? If so, where does it begin?
8. Is there a coda to this piece? If so, where does it begin?
9. In this rondo, the word *tutti* is printed at several points above the music. What does this mean?

Assignment 29

Rondo from Piano Sonata No. 37 *Haydn (1732-1809)*

1. In which key does Haydn write this Rondo?
2. How would you describe the accompaniment to the rondo theme at the beginning of the piece? Is it made up of:
    (i) patterns of broken chords?
    (ii) chords played lightly, off the main beat?
    (iii) imitation between the right hand and left hand?
3. At which bar does the first episode (B) begin?
4. In which key is episode B?
5. What contrasts are there between the music of A and the music of B?
6. How does Haydn introduce a touch of humour at the end of B?
7. Where does the rondo theme return as A²?
8. Where does the second episode (C) begin?
9. Is C in the dominant, the subdominant, or the relative minor?
10. Where does the rondo theme return as A³?
11. How does Haydn vary his rondo theme upon it last appearance?
12. Each section of this Rondo is a complete binary or ternary design in miniature. In which of these forms is the rondo theme itself?
13. Between which sections of this Rondo does Haydn write a link?
14. Where does Haydn make use of *syncopation* – a rhythmic effect in which notes are emphasised off the beat?
15. Haydn heads his music *Presto, ma non troppo*. What does this mean?

8 Variation form, & the Ground Bass

Variation form is one of the oldest musical designs, dating back to the very beginnings of instrumental music. It became very popular in the 16th century, particularly with the keyboard composers of Tudor England, and has remained a favourite form up to the present day.

As a theme, the composer chooses a fairly simple, easy-to-remember tune, often binary or ternary in design. It may be a well-known tune, such as a folk-tune; or a melody of the composer's own invention; or even a tune borrowed from another composer. The theme is first presented in a comparatively straightforward way. Then the composer builds up his music by repeating the tune as many times as he likes – but each time varying, or altering, it in some way:

A Theme	A' Variation 1	A" Variation 2	A''' Variation 3

(and so on)

The actual number of ways in which a composer may vary his theme is countless – limited only by the extent of his musical imagination. But here are the most important ones:

(a) Decorating the tune, so that it may be 'hidden' among trills, ornaments and passing notes.

(b) A change of harmony.

(c) A change of rhythm.

(d) A change of metre. For instance, three beats to a bar may be changed to four.

(e) A change of speed, or *tempo*.

(f) A change to the opposite mode – presenting the melody in the parallel major or minor key.

(g) The theme may be put down into the bass, or into an inner part.

(h) Presenting the theme, or part of the theme, in *imitation* or *canon* – rather like a round such as *Frère Jacques* – in which one vocal or instrumental part sets off with the tune, then another joins in with the same tune soon afterwards.

(i) The melody itself may actually disappear, but the harmonies or the rhythm are kept, so that we are strongly reminded of the original tune.

(j) A counter-melody may be played above or below the theme, or a new melody take its place above the original harmonies.

(k) The theme may be turned upside down (called *inversion*); or the notes stretched out into longer values (*augmentation*); or given in shorter values (*diminution*).

(l) If the music is for orchestra – a marked change of instrumentation.

A *coda* may be added to the final variation to round off the whole piece. Or the final variation may itself serve as a coda.

Occasionally, a set of variations ends with something rather more elaborate, such as a *fugue*. Or the composer may simply choose to restate his theme in exactly the same way as when it was first heard.

Sets of variations composed before the 19th century consist mainly of *decorating* the theme in various ways – disguising it with trills and ornaments, running passages and arpeggios. But later composers – Beethoven and Brahms in particular – often choose to probe deeper by *developing* the theme. 'Developing' means building up the music by working out the various melodic, rhythmic and harmonic possibilities of a musical idea. In this way, a whole variation may be built up from a single important idea taken from the theme – perhaps a fragment of melody, or a distinctive snatch of rhythm.

Now listen to how Mozart varies a rather well-known tune. Here is the theme, then the beginning of each variation, from a set he composed upon the French tune known as *Ah, vous dirai-je, Maman.*

Theme The well-known tune, in ternary form, is presented in the most straightforward way above a simple bass line. (The most important notes of the theme are marked with circles.)

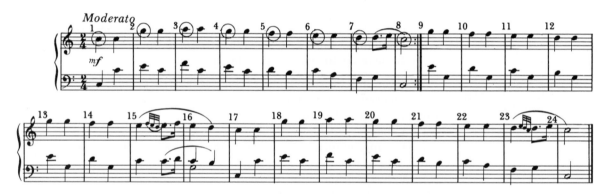

Variation 1 The theme is hidden away among swiftly running semiquavers.

Variation 2 The semiquavers pass down to the left hand while the theme is clearly heard in the right.

Variation 3 Triplets (three quavers in the time of two) disguise the theme.

etc.

Variation 4 The triplets move down to the bass as the theme is heard in firm chords for the right hand.

etc.

Variation 5 A change of rhythm: the steady crotchets of the theme are replaced first by ♩ ⁊ ♪ later by ♩ ⁊ ♫

etc.

Variation 6 The theme in full chords, riding above rushing semiquavers. After
the double bar, the theme is heard in the middle of the texture
as the semiquavers soar above into the right hand.

Variation 7 At first, the theme seems to have disappeared! But we are strongly
reminded of it by the harmonies.

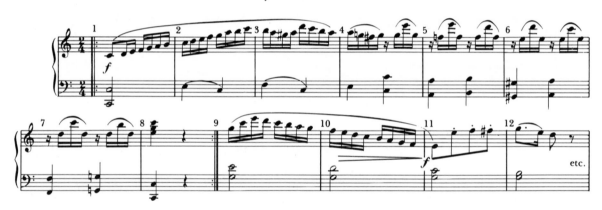

Variation 8 The theme, transformed into the minor mode, is treated in imitation.
The harmonies after the double bar are made much richer.

Variation 9 A return to the major, with the first part of the theme in imitation. Towards the end of this variation, the theme is inverted (turned upside down).

Variation 10 An exciting variation in which the theme is played by the left hand crossing over the right.

Variation 11 A change of tempo to *adagio* (slowly) for a serene, richly decorated version of the theme. Again, there is a great deal of imitation.

Variation 12 A dramatic change of tempo to *allegro* (fairly fast) and a change of metre from two beats in a bar to three. A short *coda* is added to this variation to round off the whole piece.

The Ground Bass In the 16th and 17th centuries, a type of a variation writing was very popular, called the *ground bass.* In this, the theme - or ground - is repeated over and over again in the bass, while above, the composer weaves a continuous, varying texture of melody and harmonies.

Sometimes, the divisions of the ground bass are overlapped by the melody above, binding the whole texture closely together. In some pieces, the composer makes the upper parts gradually more complicated, building up more tension as the music progresses. A ground bass is sometimes called a *basso ostinato,* meaning a bass which is 'obstinately repeated'.

The ground bass was especially popular with the English composer, Henry Purcell. There are several examples in his vocal music, but here is one of four 'Grounds' he composed for keyboard.

Ground in C Minor

Purcell (1659-1695)

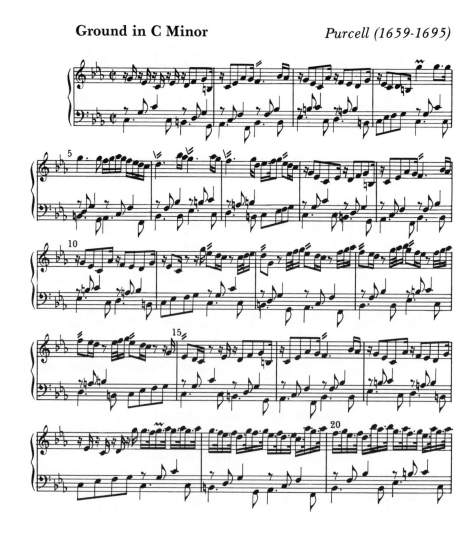

Assignment 30

1. In Purcell's *Ground in C minor*, how long is the ground itself?
2. How many times is the ground heard during this piece?

The Passacaglia and the Chaconne

Two other types of 'continuous' variations based on the *ostinato* ('obstinately repeating') idea are the *passacaglia* and the *chaconne*. Originally, both of these were dances in slow triple time. Musicians (including composers!) have always been confused about the actual difference between them. Basically, however, passacaglia is variations upon an ostinato theme which is usually found in the bass – though it may be transferred to an upper part; a chaconne is variations upon an ostinato idea which is really a chain of harmonies rather than an actual tune or melody.

Bach's great *Passacaglia in C minor* for organ consists of twenty continuous variations upon an eight-bar ostinato theme:

Listen to Bach's *Passacaglia*, then answer these questions:

Assignment 31

1. Do the variations begin immediately, or is the ostinato theme heard first alone?
2. In which variation is the rhythm of the theme first altered?
3. Is the ostinato theme transferred to the treble at any time during this Passacaglia, or does it remain always in the bass?

Assignment 32 Prélude to *L'Arlésienne* *Bizet (1838-1875)*

In 1872, the Vaudeville Theatre in Paris decided to stage a play by
Alphonse Daudet called *L'Arlésienne*. Bizet was invited to compose
some incidental music – pieces to introduce the scenes, or to be
played between scenes when the scenery was being changed.

 This *Prélude* is played before the curtain rises, and sets the
mood for the whole play. Bizet writes variations on an old
Provençal carol, called *Marcho dei Rei* (March of the Kings).

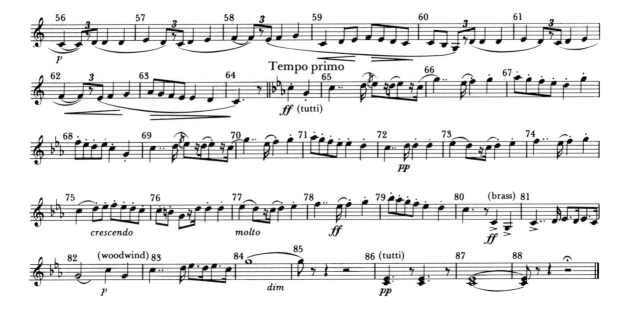

1. What is the tonic key of this music?
2. Describe how Bizet first presents his theme.
3. Is the theme binary, or ternary?
4. In which bar does Variation 1 begin?
5. Which immediate contrasts do you notice between the presentation of the theme and the music of Variation 1?
6. Where does Variation 2 begin?
7. Mention two ways in which Bizet whips up excitement in this variation.
8. Variation 3 is marked *andantino*. Is this faster, or slower, than *andante?*
9. Which instruments play the melody in Variation 3?
10. Two pairs of instruments can be heard in the background – one pair playing a running accompaniment; the other pair playing a smoother, more flowing line. Which instruments make up these pairs?
11. Several changes are made to the theme in the third variation. List as many of them as you can.
12. Variation 4 is marked *tempo primo*. What does this mean?
13. How does Bizet vary his theme here?
14. Which musical term describes bars 80 to 88?
15. Which of these variations is written in a contrasting key? Which key is it?
16. Which of the variations do you find the most interesting? Why?
17. What nationality was Bizet?
18. Name any other music by Bizet which you have heard.

Assignment 33

Theme with Variations

Schumann (1810-1856)

1. In which key is the theme?
2. The pace marking is *poco lento*. What does this mean?
3. In which variation is in the theme heard in the bass?
4. Which variation is in the tonic major key? Which key is this?
5. In which variation is the theme heard in the middle of the texture?
6. In which variation is a counter-melody added above the theme?
7. Describe how the theme is varied in Variation 5.
8. Is the Coda in any way based on the theme? Or is it built from entirely new musical material?

Assignment 34
'Thème Slave Varié' from the ballet *Coppélia*   *Delibes (1836-1891)*

There are five variations on this ternary theme. Listen to the music carefully, and see if you can match the correct description (given below) to each of the variations. A link joins two of the variations: strings are cheekily imitated by woodwind - at one point sounding like orchestral laughter. The variations end with a coda in which the trombones twice remind us of the opening bars of the theme. Then the entire orchestra brings the piece to an exciting conclusion.

Cellos and low woodwind take the theme, as the violins race briskly up and down.

The theme is disguised by swift, light and rhythmic strings. In A², brass and cymbals are important.

Full orchestra: strongly rhythmic chords, answered by crisp woodwind. Cymbals are added in A².

A¹ is played by clarinets, while strings and high woodwind add impudent comments. B is given to the oboes.

A change of pace and metre (three beats to a bar instead of two) for a melancholy clarinet solo above a hesitant string accompaniment.

Assignment 35

Dido's Lament, from *Dido and Aeneas*   *Purcell (1659-1695)*

Dido and Aeneas is Purcell's only opera. Dido, Queen of
Carthage, falls deeply in love with Aeneas, who has been driven
to her shores during a violent storm. But Aeneas is tricked by
witchcraft into deserting her. Dido, her heart broken, sings
this lament as she is dying.

1. How many bars long is the ground upon which Purcell builds up this music?
2. How many times is the ground heard during the piece?
3. Between which playings of the ground does Purcell overlap the voice part, carrying the music forward by a smooth joining of the 'seams'?
4. Which type of voice sings this lament?
5. Which instruments play the accompaniment?

9

Special Assignment B

Each of these five pieces is in binary, ternary, minuet and trio, variation, or simple rondo form. As before, your assignment is to investigate each piece and discover which form the composer has used to build up his music.

1. Note down all the important features of each piece, such as:
   (i)   bar numbers where sections begin and end;
   (ii) the key scheme used;
   (iii) any striking contrasts, or similarities, between sections;
   (iv) interesting choice of instruments, and so on.
2. Add as many important facts as you can about each composer.
3. Make out a plan, or draw a diagram, clearly showing the form of each piece, using the letters A, B, and so on, and giving the bar numbers for each section.
4. Finally, organise your findings into a detailed report on each piece.

1 'Dance of the Cygnets' from the ballet *Swan Lake*   *Tchaikovsky (1840-1893)*

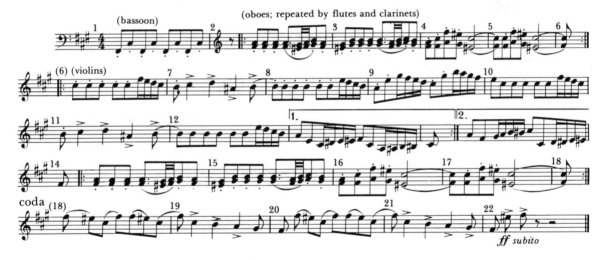

2 German Dance   *Schubert (1797-1828)*

3 Third Movement from Bassoon Concerto

Mozart (1756-1791)

4 **Choral**

Bartók (1881-1945)

5 Slow Movement of the Concerto 'Winter' from *The Four Seasons*   *Vivaldi (1678-1741)*

6 Third Movement from the 'Drumroll' Symphony   *Haydn (1732-1809)*